The Weight of Whiteness

The Weight of Whiteness

A Memoir in Poetry

by **Caroline Giles Banks**

WELLINGTON-GILES PRESS

Minneapolis, Minnesota

United States of America

WELLINGTON-GILES PRESS
4040 Sheridan Avenue South
Minneapolis, Minnesota 55410
United States of America
wellingtongilespress@gmail.com

Book design by Cate Hubbard

Library of Congress Control Number : 2012905890

ISBN 978-0-9645254-2-9
eBook ISBN 978-0-9645254-3-6

Acknowledgements

The following poems were first published in the magazines and anthologies noted below, some in slightly modified form. Copyright © by Caroline Giles Banks.

"Harriet Tubman" in *2000, Here's to Humanity*, edited by Shirley Richburg, The People's Press, 1999. Also published in *Anthropology and Humanism*, Volume 24, Number 2, 1999.

"What's in a Name" originally published under the title "Name-Dropping" in *Asheville Poetry Review*, Volume 3, Number 1, 1996. Also published under the title "Logan" in *Re-Imagining Naming*, edited by Nancy J. Berneking, Volume 29, November 2001, and in "Family Ties," *Verve*, edited by Marilyn Hochheiser, Volume 9, Number 2, 1997.

"View from Space" in *Full Circle Twenty-Seven*, edited by Leon Knight, Guild Press, Robbinsdale, Minnesota, 2006.

"Sphinx" in *Full Circle Twenty*, edited by Leon Knight, Guild Press, Robbinsdale, Minnesota, 1999. Also published in *Forced from the Garden, Poetry and Short Prose by Women*, Guild Press, Robbinsdale, Minnesota, 2003.

"Hair" in *Asheville Poetry Review*, Volume 3, Number 1, 1996.

"Baby Shower" in *Full Circle Twenty-Seven*, edited by Leon Knight, Guild Press, Robbinsdale, Minnesota, 2006.

"My Southern Cousins" in *Rockhurst Review 2006: A Fine Arts Journal*, edited by Patricia Miller, Kansas City, Missouri, 2006.

"Vital Records" in *Joining the Circle 2007*, edited by George D. Clabon, TA Publications, Minneapolis, Minnesota, 2007. Also published in *Full Circle Twenty-Eight*, edited by Leon Knight, Guild Press, Robbinsdale, Minnesota, 2007.

"So Now They Burn a Cross in Her Yard" in *Wisconsin Dialogue*, Volume 10, 1990.

"Victoria Falls, Zambia" in *Wisconsin Dialogue*, Volume 10, 1990. Also in *Full Circle Twenty-Nine*, edited by Leon Knight, Guild Press, Robbinsdale, Minnesota, 2008.

"Caprices on the Carnation" in *Re-Imagining*, edited by Nancy Berneking, Volume 28, August 2001.

"All God's Children" in *Full Circle Twenty-Eight*, edited by Leon Knight, Guild Press, Robbinsdale, Minnesota, 2007.

"Christmas With Texas Grandparents" in *Full Circle Twenty-Nine*, edited by Leon Knight, Guild Press, Robbinsdale, Minnesota, 2008.

"Playground Language Lesson" in *Full Circle Twenty-Nine*, edited by Leon Knight, Guild Press, Robbinsdale, Minnesota, 2008.

"Boxes" in *Full Circle Twenty-Nine*, edited by Leon Knight, Guild Press, Robbinsdale, Minnesota, 2008.

"Back of the Church" in *Full Circle Twenty-Eight*, edited by Leon Knight, Guild Press, Robbinsdale, Minnesota, 2007.

Many thanks to Joan Kanavich and Cate Hubbard for providing technical support in bringing the book to its final form. Juliet Patterson, Joan Drury, Marc Burgett, and Leon Knight gave me valued editorial comments. And Claire McInerney, Kathleen Kuehnast, and Judy Hornbacher encouraged me to perservere.

For

Roger, Logan, Tyler, and Madison

Contents

What is the weight of whiteness?
Beneath the pale surface
drags the blue-black underside—
fathomless grief,
unseen connections.

❖

I

...sexuality remains a widely acknowledged

core of the race problem. Miscegenation

is indeed the most forbidden of interracial

practices —

Joel Kovel in
White Racism

Welcome to the USA

After a month in Rotterdam,
time enough for their new VW
to get to New York City by boat,
they clear customs,
present paperwork at the docks,
drive West in twilight rain.
At a tollbooth between New York
and New Jersey, the lone attendant, burly
and pasty under Hopperesque fluorescent
lights, stares at his steel gray
beard, her smooth baby Gouda skin.
Fearing he'll issue a pass
to a federal felony
if he raises the gate,
the guard hesitates,
asks if she is okay.
Nodding, she pulls up her jacket sleeve,
shows him her burnished gold ring.

Vital Records

Packing up to move
to our new home
I see the birth certificate
in his box of premarital mementos.

Date: 1936
Place: Santa Fe, New Mexico
Race: White

White?
How could the Registrar of Vital Records
make such a mistake?
He is browner than the bricks
of our adobe house
under the cottonwood trees.
Anyone who sees us sees
I am the white one
in this union.
Stunned, curious,
I brandish the document so
out of synch
with my color wheel.
Standing among the empty boxes
he tells me,
Santa Fe's black population
was minuscule before the war,
my dad and uncle bartenders at La Fonda,
our neighbors porters for the railroad.

Our families clustered
along the Alameda in a compound
Uncle Harold called "Chinatown."
In a state with so few blacks
a baby born off the Rez
without a Hispanic last name
would be Anglo, White.
Wouldn't my colleagues in the Urban League,
N.A.A.C.P., Afro-American Studies
laugh themselves silly
if they knew?

Ode to Ray Charles Robinson
(after seeing the film, *Ray*)

Ray
Ray Charles
Ray Charles Robinson!
Your ramped-up gospel sound
shot straight to my veins in Dallas, 1963,
fire searing the stony-faced analyst
sitting mute in a dimmed room.
But, Ray, the film didn't get it right.
Blacks and whites
weren't dancing together
in the aisles that night.
Jim Crow ushered *Coloreds*
to the back of the balcony—
nigger heaven—then.
And white girls like me
wore kid gloves to dances,
safely sequestered
in private clubs and schools.
The closest
we were allowed
to blacks
were silent servants
with no last names.
O Ray
Ray Charles
Ray Charles Robinson!
The way you tilted your face

toward heaven when you sang
riffed on a longing
for connection in my soul.
Are you why
a few years later
I broke laws, my parents' hearts,
and ran off with a man
like you?

Courtship

1

Navigating the freckles on my skin
      with the tips of your fingers
            you trace constellations on my body:

the Big Dipper on my right thigh,
      taut Archer's bow on my forearms,
            Venus and Mars between my breasts.

Your hand mines my heart,
      a plain geode exploding to reveal
            a white crystalline world within.

2

Picking the rubies
      from their waxy comb,
            you place the jewels
                  on my tongue,

show me how
      to press the seeds
            to the roof
                of my mouth.

My lips stain red.

Each swallow
       breaks me
              from my father,
                     my mother,

binds me to you—
       Persephone to Pluto—
              for our future life.

3

You appear at my front door,
       your Afro tight from the summer rain,
              an ice cream cone hardly
                     dripping over your hand.

Carless then,
       you winged it
              from the sweetshop
                     six blocks away.

How can I resist?
       One lick
              bolts me
                     to you.

Painted Men

They honeymoon, post-elopement, in Spain,
far from the States
still roiling from the movement
to eat a burger at Woolworth's,
to sit in
the front of the bus.
She is young, thinks
Europeans will be blind
to the mixed colors
of their skin.
He is older, like Baldwin a veteran abroad,
knows the stares he got in India
serving in the Peace Corps
were because he's American,
not dark.
Barcelona.
Midnight.
Too much New Year's Eve champagne.
The gorgeous blond, expat Swede,
fawns her hands
over his face,
says, so the new bride hears,
I love painted men.
This night an older battle:
sex
trumps nationality, color,
and race.

Love vs.
(after Sherman Alexie)

This is a poem for all couples who defy boundaries.

This is a poem for the black/white couple in Virginia who wanted
to marry but the law forbade it.

This is a poem for their love and lawyers who sued Virginia before
the U.S. Supreme Court.

This is a poem for the Justices who, in 1967, declared unconstitutional
sixteen states' laws prohibiting mixed race marriages.

This is a poem for the Constitution and its defenders.

This is a poem for the young black/white couple from the East
who came to teach poor whites in West Texas and fled
when the local sheriff peeped in their window.

This is a poem for the illiterate police who couldn't read
about the South's new rules of engagement.

This is a poem for the Justice of the Peace in Santa Fe who asked me if
I knew what I was doing before he married us in 1966. Did he think
I was pregnant, that this was a shotgun wedding, but without
parents and guns?

This is a poem for naiveté.

This is a poem for the old VW bus with no reverse gear
that carried us from JP to JP.

This is a poem for the wild flowers I picked along the road
for my bridal bouquet.

This is a poem for Barney and Luce Hopewell, our witnesses.

This is a poem for optimistic-sounding last names.

This is a poem for the woman in the bar who gave us the finger
for a wedding toast.

This is a poem for my father in Dallas who got roaring drunk
after he got the news.

This is a poem for my Episcopalian mother who insisted we meet
with the Dean of the Cathedral in Albuquerque. She wanted
the church to bless our ungodly union. To bring me to my senses.
To report back to her about Roger's character.

This is a poem for the Dean who served with Roger on the same
Community Action Board in the War on Poverty. He reported to my
mother that Roger was an upstanding citizen. For years she sent Roger
the Sunday *Times* because he, too, liked doing the crossword puzzle.

This is a poem for the liberal wing of the Anglican Communion.

This is a poem for the rednecks with loaded rifle racks who rode our
back bumper when we drove from Albuquerque to Flagstaff, Arizona.

This is a poem for all the landlords who said the apartment was no longer available.

This is a poem for the Hispanic landlady in Albuquerque who rented to us to annoy the snooty Anglo neighbors.

This is a poem for snooty neighbors and righteous landladies.

This is a poem for Roger who drove us up to Taos for a gourmet French meal, gave me a dozen red roses and a Happy 50th card in celebration of our surviving one year together.

This is a poem for small steps forward, even if each seems to take half a century.

Lineage

Tribal elder stamping his staff
for attention to his story,
my father-in-law sits
on the edge of his chair,
legs spread wide, holding
a golf club straight upside down
between his knees.

My father worked in the Colorado mines.
We were rag poor, an apple
or orange my gift on Christmas morning.
Mother had aspirations for us boys, taught us
Latin, but we dropped school at fourteen
to join father underground.

He touches on former wives
with flower names—
Violet, Iris—then, to Italy
serving in a segregated platoon
freeing Europeans from tyranny,
only to work for tips
as club waiter, bartender
when he got back home.

One night when I was little
I overheard Mother and Grandmother
whispering behind the bed curtains
that my great-grandmother was
a princess

snatched by a slave trader
from her kingdom home
in Madagascar.

Looking straight into my hazel eyes,
he pauses.
His silent stare says,
Your husband is royalty.
You are the one
who married "up."

Links Luncheon

(Phoenix, mid-1960s)

Just freed
>   from my mother's
>>   post–World War II hats, gloves, girdles,

my miniskirt above
>   my pale knees,
>>   I'm a specimen of women's lib

for my new mother-in-law's
>   veiled-in-Sunday-best
>>   friends to scrutinize.

At the luncheon
>   I'm seated with Charlesetta,
>>   Winstona, Marquelyn,

women's names,
>   names with expectations
>>   given long before

Freidan and Steinem excited
>   white women to burn
>>   our bras, get MBAs.

Many, like my mother-in-law,
>   teach in the city's
>>   still segregated schools,

each year paying cash
     for Cadillacs,

the banks' redlines
     keeping them from
          drawing their salaries

for homes with lawns,
     pools, good schools.

And they invest in their exodus,
     add to their portfolios
          of teardown properties

soon to be sought
     for more runways,
          the bulging downtown.

The woman on my left,
     whose husband owns mortuaries,
          a fleet of ambulances,

grows and arranges funereal flowers
     for their monopoly on
          the business of black death.

When she hints her husband
     cooks the evening meal,
          changes the baby,
               scrubs the kitchen floor,

I sense my recent crossing
        of the color line

means I'm to be liberated
        from my mother's housewifery
                without a struggle, strike.

And they are just as thrilled
        to be served luncheon
                for the first time

in the banquet room
        of a fancy downtown hotel.

Wedding Portrait
(1966)

Roger wears a badass Afro, shades,
and the *dashiki* I made from a pattern
and cloth begrudgingly sold
to us in Oakland after the riots.
The shopkeeper asked Roger
how he could support the movement
with me in the picture.
Man, where are you from?
I'm in a yellow *Marimekko* dress—
Finnish for "little Mary"—
my head veiled in late summer thunderclouds
coming towards the Rio Grande valley
somewhere between Taos and Albuquerque.
A hitchhiker filmmaker from LA
doing a piece on a hippie commune
shot us at a roadside rest,
the glossy print our only elopement portrait.

How could I know
our marriage was going to be more
than just us?
I was clueless about sex,
the politics of sex.
I did not know
across the border in Texas
our marriage was illegal.

We could be arrested, barred
from crossing the line together
if troopers had a mind
to. Actors and artists, diehard Socialists,
ex-Peace Corps volunteers back from Columbia—
our friends—said we were cool, courageous.
With a gold band
I became a radical,
learned to use race
to make a cover story
of why I married
a man who was wrong
for me,
who drank
himself to blackouts,
terrified me
when he thrust his Special Forces fist
through the bedroom ceiling
in a PTSD nightmare,
a man I pitied,
thought I could rescue.
It took years
to step outside
the frame of this photo,
to go beneath the colors
of our skin.
Roger says he thought
we wouldn't last
a year.

Chagall Triptych

1

Lovers in the Lilacs, 1930

Pink and white lilacs,
unmoored from dirt, vase, hands,
float above the horizon.
Fragrance balloons the bouquet
to dwarf the moon,
reduce the village to a spire.
A couple lies bedded
in this ether beyond
gravity.

2

L'Obsession, 1943

A crucifix crushes a Jew
holding three candles of death.
Skies stain red,
synagogues collapse in ashes.
Families pile in carts
harnessed to horses frozen
blue with shock.
Young wives wear widow's black,
barren by madness.

3

Couple on a Red Background, 1983

An acrobat balances
on the cock of a new day.
Rows of red houses corral
a white and green synagogue standing
whole on a hill.
Their bodies tethered to the ground,
a couple embraces in a golden meadow.
Pink and white lilacs float
in the cool blue pool of memory.
Here, palette and body are tempered twins,
the artist's hope for humankind
mature beyond division or despair.

Forever Dead in Eurydice

Be forever dead in Eurydice—more gladly arise
into the seamless life proclaimed in your song.

Rilke

1

They meet
in the student union
between classes:
he—handsome brown, jazz drummer;
she—just out
of a posh women's college
somewhere in the East,
greenhouse green, still
a believer in tales.
He takes her
to see *Orpheo Negro*, filmed
in black and white.
Her memory says everything
from then on
was black and white.
With an arm around her shoulder
he brings her into their story.

2

Rio. Carnival.
He—beautiful musician, poet,
moves beasts, even
rocks, trees with his song.
She—tall-and-fair-and-young-
and-lovely. They dance
into it.

3

Santa Fe. Festival. Mid-sixties.
Zozobra, Old Man Gloom, explodes
firecrackers from his mouth,
roaring light.
Their loneliness collapses.
They elope in a VW bus.
She carries black-eyed susans,
wild, like her.

4

She is snatched down under
by a rival
for her love, masked
in skeletal bones.
Her husband, grieving,
descends spiral after
spiral into the pit
of it. Past Charon, past Cerberus,
past the Judges
of the Dead.
Told not to look
at her face,
how can he resist
turning backward
for a glance?
They burn
in a love
that must see, cannot
not be.

5

Learning of her marriage
to a *colored man,*
her parents cut her
off, her old friends stop
stopping by.
Perplexed by her paralysis,
stuck between
familial love and marital passion,
even he stops
playing for her.
No one comes
searching. She wanders
between, beyond
black and white.
How lonely
this love without
color, without face.

My Southern Cousins

Do they see me
as a Desdemona
heading straight into tragedy
of Shakespearean proportions?

Do they think
he made me do it,
cast a spell
with stories of his adventures
among the *anthropophegi*?

Am I
a sharp-faced matron
on the Underground Railroad,
a New England–born freedom rider,
an N.A.A.C.P. activist
making a statement?

When I broke the taboo
all eight girl cousins
below the Mason-Dixon
were sequestered
in schools safe
in the Deep South
with house mothers, house rules,
and no chance
of falling into my story.

                              How do they tell
my story?
Outcast at family gatherings,
I have never heard
how they talk
about me. Words unheard
keep me in silent shadow,
ghostly consort
to one of America's
invisible men.

Cruel Truth of Sleep

She walks
into my backyard
(it is summer, everything
is vivid, green)
finally coming to visit,
finally after twenty-five years
of excuses,
and collapses
face down
in the grass.
I watch,
say nothing,
do nothing,
in the paralysis
of dream.
In a haze
someone (in this story
only she and I
are real)
covers her.
With the tuck
of a blanket
she is gone.
I have killed my mother.

The Day of the Rope

**(as described in *The Turner Diaries*,
bible of the extremist right)**

If they have their way
they would dangle us
from utility poles,
all the pale-skinned women
who broke their taboo.

Who counts and marks us?
White supremacists hunkered down
in backwoods enclaves,
boundaries staked
with Confederate flags,
pro-life billboards?
How do they identify us,
the numerous pale petals
tenderly opened
by dark fingers and lips
to bear wondrous
and strange fruit?

They aren't interested
in a precise tally,
only instilling fear
to keep the stock pure.
Placards around our necks will read,
I defiled my race
on *The Day of the Rope.*

And they will nuke the rest,
our brown husbands and lovers,
sons and daughters,
while they, *true* believers,
will be raptured to heaven
while the world below burns.

May the blast
(and, if there is a God,
please forbid the blast)
be so powerful that the "*l*" and "*my*"
scorch off the placards
and each announces:
I defied race.

So Now They Burn a Cross in Her Yard

(after Wole Soyinka's *So Now They Burn the Roof above Her Head*)

For Coretta Scott King

So now they burn a cross in her yard?
Well, it has happened before. Racist minds,
like children, never grow up. They still play
dress-up. Afraid of recognition, did
not these local officials once wear their
sheets to town?

              They wore, ironically, the
color of innocence and surrender. The
disguise encouraged them, circling in hate.
They came, they shouted, raged as rednecks
know how. They wore sheets of love,
but hate propelled them.

Their sheets, their bed sheets, she noted.
Fine linen, she taught them,
*by loving hands tended and smoothed,
they held love, with all who love and hold.*

*Those bed sheets have been bleached of love's compassion.
In wondrous sleep, they could cradle dreams
that all men and women can climb mountains
and be free. Do you not marvel then, they are
the color of peace?*

Still they wore their sheets to town, Martin—
and now they burn a cross in her yard.

Back of the Church
(Phoenix, Arizona)

Driving to church,
her uncle-in-law sings spirituals
in his down-home preacher's
(not School Superintendent's)
voice, his Bible between them.
Pulling into the lot
he turns and tells her, *wait a few minutes,*
then slip in and sit in the back pew.

Jesus, I'm no stranger here, she says.
I'm a stand-up, greet-the-congregation,
            be-seen white guest,
your sister's (their organist's) daughter-in-law.
            They know you and I are kin.

Don't matter squat, he insists.
            King's gone.
They preachin' separate, not together, now.
The brethren see me with you, I'm dead.

Secret mistress to integration
prompted to enter discreetly
through a side door,
she hesitates a few minutes—
            then goes in.

Tomb Figure I

Prajnaparamita, Goddess of Transcendental Wisdom
13th Century Cambodia
Minneapolis Institute of Arts

To you, my head seems perfection:
a little Buddha sits
at the base of the conical crown
and my mouth is finely chiseled
in an eternal smile.
Below the neck
I am crumbling.
One arm is broken
at the elbow,
the other severed
under the shoulder blade.
My missing limbs lie
far away underground.
If you look into my face
a mica tear
betrays my serenity
during centuries of plunder
that bring me here
before you.

❖

II

...language is a major medium through which

cultural difference is enacted,

expressed and maintained —

Laurence A. Hirschfield in
Race in the Making

Fragments of Things

I often painted fragments of things
because it seemed to make my statement
as well as or better than the whole could...
                                    Georgia O'Keeffe

1

Black Place III, 1944

A massive bolt of lightning splits
open the black-gray mountains
near Los Alamos.
Her eye sees
the blinding light, clouds of fire
coming over the mountains.
Her mind knows
the secret labs made a bomb
that surpasses the lightning's strike
to make the black place.

2

Pelvis IV, 1944

          Still the war.
The morning moon,
blue sky,
are seen—like everything—
through bleached, dry bone.

3

January, 1944

        Born
under the shadow
of the A-bomb, I learn
to seek shelter
under a desk, to fear
the black place,
fragments of things,
bone.

Awakenings

1 Boston Irish

You were three or four.
We were walking downtown when
a colored woman approached us.
You went right up to her, said,
"How now, brown cow?"

My first encounter with a black person.
I grab a line
from my Irish grandmother's lexicon:
the best solution to an unexpected arrival
is to have a drink
from the *"brown cow,"*
a barrel of beer!

2 Hidey-Hole

Seven or eight.
Boston.
Elementary school field trip
visiting houses
used in the Underground Railroad,
each with a secret room—
windowless, stale,
small as a casket—
I suck in my breath
when told how many
runaways each held.

Before the long summer vacation
I help Mother
hide jewelry, family sterling
from urban burglars and thieves.
She parts jackets and coats
hanging in the closet
tucked under the front hall stairs
of our old New England home,
pries open a panel wall.
Staring down into a dirt hole
size enough for a family to crouch,
I imagine
a hair ribbon, rag doll,
quilt scrap, crude map,
and know this cellar of dreams
and escape held cargo more precious
than Mother's spoons and pearls.

3 Brown vs. the Board of Education

Boston.
Mid-fifties.
Hicks, school superintendent,
forces integration, incites
riots in Roxbury.
Oblivious to race politics,
I bike after school
to my new classmate's apartment,
the fire escape entrance,
crowded kitchen/bath/bedroom for nine,
so exotic, new.
My friend and her brothers,
kinky, boisterous,
come to my house
and Mother accuses them
of stealing change
from a kitchen drawer,
bans any future play.
Weeks later
I'm whisked off
to a private school
without blacks, boys,
two towns
and a carpool away.
I know Mother
and I have forever parted ways.

4 Christmas with Texas Grandparents

The heyday of trains,
we travel North to South for days,
cut colored paper chains
several cars long
to hang from Grandma's tree.
I am old enough to see
the porters' dark skin pass
from stares to invisibility
by our final whistle stop. In Dallas
we are left with Lucy and Ellihue
who say how tall we've gotten.
Lucy rolls out crust at her large marble top table,
while Ellihue rakes pecans for the pie.
During dinner Grandma presses her foot
on the buzzer hidden
under the dining room carpet,
her signal for Ellihue,
in white jockey jacket and gloves,
to pass around holiday dishes.
Grandpa urges us to seconds, thirds,
stuffs us to long naps.
After leftovers taken in whispers
on kitchen stools
Lucy and Ellihue walk
to their room above the garage.
I beg Grandma to see them.
With a, *no,*

I learn about domestic relations
in this land of Jim Crow:
Blacks can enter Grandma's house,
cook our food, bathe and tease me,
but I am forbidden
to enter their world.

5 Family Vacation

Driving back to the motel,
stifling in the 90-degree Florida heat,
Dad tells us
in his, *don't ask questions, just do it*, tone
to lock the doors,
roll up the windows fast.
We rock up on our knees,
see through the dusty glass
dozens of black men
in white and black
striped jackets and pants,
ankle tethered to ankle,
a chorus of sledge hammers
tightly choreographed by armed troopers
idling on high horses.
Lung-pounding pressure to perform
in synchronized unison.
Fettered thirst, feet.
The white troopers' prancing horses
have it better than these convicts.

Caprices on the Carnation

1

From *carne*, flesh,
originally flesh-colored.
I like them red, bloodred,
the color that moves through flesh,
capillaries exploded into red.

2

The carnation, variety of *Dianthus caryophyllus,*
Old World Pink. *Dianthus,*
Latin for *Heavenly Flower*.

3

Dianthus, Diana, Artemis,
moon goddesses,
goddesses of the forest,
of childbirth.
I sleep in a room
wallpapered with small bouquets
of red carnations.
I am a child
waiting to be born.

4

I push up
through the earth's surface,
hair encrusted with postpartum sand and mud.
I hold red carnations,
born of earth, *chthonic*, like me.

5

Milk, Carnation Milk, milk
in the red and white–papered can.
Mixed with Karo Corn Syrup and water,
a sweet formula for babies.

6

Carnations are capricious. I find them
in gardens, Japanese prints, wallpaper,
note cards, museum tapestries, lapels,
on altars, in a small bouquet of flowers
in the dining room of a honeymoon inn,
bath talc, nightgowns, bed sheets.

7

Weaned from my mother's breasts
I suckle carnations from a bottle,
tight little buds and stems,
thin dark green leaves,
red double-flowered petals
that do not easily wilt.
My mouth is a garden, a perennial bouquet.
Each bud blossoms in a poem,
a kiss.

8

As a girl I hear stories
about Zina Diantha Huntington Smith Young (1821-1901)
from my grandmother and great-aunts.
The stories are cautionary tales
passed among my kin,
moral lessons about the kind of woman *not to be*.
Zina Diantha left her husband and sons
to marry Mormon leaders Joseph Smith
and Brigham Young.
She raised silkworms
and was said by my great-aunts
to be ugly.

9

First prom, first kiss.
The carnation in his lapel
presses against my strapless-bare skin,
its scent of cinnamon-cloves and
something new.

10

Zina Diantha had hazel eyes like mine
and her braids circled her head
like a crown.
Diantha:
I shall weave carnations
into garments of silk
for women, plain women,
who walk out the door
to tend their silkworms
and never come back.

11

Justice of the Peace.
Red carnation in my hair.
I choose a man against
my parents' and Southern society's
sensibilities. Like you, dear
Diantha, I walk out the door
and do not turn back.

12

Communion.
Red carnations on the altar.
I pray, *dear goddess, no more*
little crucifixions, my "I wants"
hung on the hook
of denial where they die,
ascend to heaven, and become
"Thou shalt not haves." My womb
aches. I want
a *this* world communion, skin
on skin.

13

Incarnation. Incarnate:
realization of the divine in bodily form.
His bare back touches Jupiter, Mars,
Venus, Uranus, and, yes, the moon.
My back presses into Great Mother,
soft, fertile, and warm.
Incarnation.

14

This is my will:
red carnations
scattered with my ashes
around a hidden Quetico lake,
accessible only by canoe.
I want a flotilla of muscled paddlers, all
the lovers with devotion
and a good sense of direction,
paddling canoes full of me
and red carnations.

✠

III

It is a peculiar sensation, this

double-consciousness, this sense of

always looking at one's self through

the eyes of others, of measuring one's

soul by the tape of a world that looks

on in amused contempt and pity.

One ever feels his twoness—an

American, a Negro; two souls, two thoughts,

two unreconciled strivings; two warring

ideals in one dark body, whose dogged

strength alone keeps it from being

torn asunder.

W.E.B. DuBois in
The Souls of Black Folk

Baby Shower

Elders initiating a novice,
       the women,
wearing shirtwaist dresses,
matching hats and pocketbooks,
crowd around the crib inspecting
       my son.
The baby's hair will be good,
       not nappy,
       they say.
Be sure to oil his skin
so it won't get ashy.
Staring at the baby photo on the dresser
of my son's paternal step-grandmother—
herself childless—
the women repeat the nursery's party line:
the babies look exactly alike.
The boy, they whisper, *is*
       her name child.
I've given my barren in-law
a longed-for *spirit child.*

Baby's Milk

She nurses the baby
while her in-laws eat
fried chicken,
greens with fatback and sugar,
airy white bread.
Butch, just out of Morehouse,
slams his greasy napkin on the table,
plants himself, legs spread apart,
in front of her.
With a Mau Mau stare
their envoy tells her
she's starving the baby to death.
Ain't nothin'
in that thin, pale gray milk of yours.
Hand over the boy.
We'll give him a bottle, real food,
make him a man.

It's the early '70s.
White girls like her are into La Leche,
home-baked brown bread,
boycotting Nestle, table grapes.
Digging in against the united chorus
for their formula of feeding
she lifts up her blouse,
presses the baby to her breast.

Later, back home,
the baby's stool turns red.
The doctor asks,
are you feeding him solids,
anything new?
Sheepishly her husband confesses
he's slipping him formula
laced with bodybuilder's Tiger's Milk,
family orders,
to wean him off her breast.

Tomb Figure II

Mother and Child
20th Century Yombe (Democratic Republic of Congo)
Minneapolis Institute of Arts

My boy-child lies on my lap.
His head, resting in the palm of my left hand,
turns from my pendulous breasts.
Before fleeing the fighting
we sat on the earthen graves
of our Yombe ancestors,
bringing fertility and honor
to our clan. Here,
in a sealed box of metal and glass,
we sit alone before you.
The air grows stale and
I am afraid.
I wear all my power
to keep alive the link
between Yombe past and Yombe future:
a necklace of six canine teeth,
black spots on my orange-brown body,
a blacker tattoo in the small of my back.
But I am terrified
this will not be enough
to make you hear my cries
for my limp boy-child.

View From Space

He thinks of a continent:
       the one seen in photos
       shot from the moon;
the one shaped like a vast real heart;
the one where eons ago it all began;
       the one plundered
of our bodies, dreams, and gold;
       the one broken off,
       rifted from the rest;
the one where tears are immeasurable
as the Zambezi over Victoria Falls;
       the one where I am drowning
       and his shadow falls.

Playground Language Lesson

He is three or four,
oscillating between wanting
underdogs on the swing
and playing on the slide
with the big boys.
They are six or seven,
gaping holes in their smiles,
little chests puffed out
under baggy T-shirts
as they flex pink arms
to compare muscles.
They must have wanted to get him
off their backs.

*Mom, what is a **nicker**?*

My mind tumbles down
the list of words
preschoolers might be learning:
nickel, nick, nickname.
Grasping, with desire to teach:

***Knickers** are baggy pants*
with a tight band under the knee.
Golfers like Granddad used to pair them
with long socks, diamond-patterned sweater vests,
hats with pompoms on the top.

*No, Mom, what is a **nicker**?*
The big boys say
*I'm a **nicker**.*

Juxtaposition

Nobody Around Here Calls Me Citizen, 1943
by Robert Gwathmey, Weisman Art Museum
University of Minnesota, Minneapolis, Minnesota

The blackest black man,
arms folded across
his shrunken chest
like the possibility of an equal sign,
stands before a wall
with the number **"2"**
in red paint, in my mind,
read to,
sign of the shuttered schools
of segregation.
A lion, tribal totem,
front paw and tail raised,
eyes piercing and mouth open,
ready to roar and strike,
shrinks inside the locked box of memory.

I want the man
to put down his rake and hat,
to learn to read
about his roots in a continent
where mere centuries ago
his ancestors ruled kingdoms
and even lions were free,

to step to his left
and cover the number
until it
and all other rankings
are erased.

What's In a Name

When my son learned about slavery
he wanted to drop his last name,
the name of the Scotsman
who bought his dad's ancestors at auction
and worked them in the tobacco fields
before they dragged the name
to the Southwest
to labor down in the mines
or above ground in crisp white jackets
for the railroad and its chains
of hotels along the lines.

Doing a school project on family trees
my son learned that my ancestors
owned and sold slaves
and wanted to erase his middle name,
my maiden name.
My father's family, Scotsmen, too,
grew prosperous off the backs of slaves
working Virginia and Carolina soil
for cotton and tobacco.
Finding themselves on the losing side
of the Revolutionary War they fled
their plantations and titles of *General* to
Texas, Tennessee. There my ancestors willed
farmland, animals, and slaves
down the generations,

monetary value black-inked
in loopy cursive for posterity
in courthouse archives.

       In adolescence, wanting to shuck
the double shame of slavery—
owner and owned—
my son claimed the proud heritage
of his given name,
taken from his great-grandmother.
Part freeborn black, part Cherokee, graduate
of New Mexico Normal School in the late 1800s,
she helped raise Ralph Bunche,
future Nobel laureate.
In the late 1930s she went before
the Albuquerque School Board,
insisted that black children go to schools
with Hispanics and whites.
All our children deserve the same:
good teachers, good schools.

Logan Giles Banks

All God's Children

Weeks of *Ma, I don't want to go* are over.
My son will be confirmed in the Episcopal Church.
      Before the service
      a church official,
stiff white collar pinching
his neck and face Pepto Bismol–pink,
      asks if the boy has been baptized.
      There is no record, he states.
I explain about the naming ceremony,
      how when my son was little,
his great-grandfather, Reverend Favors,
      held him up
to his Black Baptist congregation,
Church Mothers' fans aflutter
      as the baby was cradled
in the reverend's outstretched arms,
      and made him "one of Jesus' own."

      Without hesitation,
      without consideration,
the Episcopal minister says,
      that ritual does not count.
      So bystanders, strangers,
      are hastened to the font,
quick words said with water
      to seal my son
to their Father, Son, and Holy Ghost.

Like a high voltage line along a boulevard
arching and bending trees apart
     the new claimant
     on my son's soul, salvation
     renders a schism
     in once common ground.

Harriet Tubman

She felt the first sting of slavery when as a young
girl she was struck on the head with an iron bar
by an enraged overseer.*

Jacob Lawrence

She is late
bringing water
to other field hands
working on Broadacres.
The buckets are so heavy,
backbreaking full.
One sharp blow to the left temple
knocks her to the ground,
banishing forever
the clear blue skies
and somersaults of girlhood.
Harriet sees two black trouser legs,
the overseer's rake-like arm
and hand—yellow-orange and
grotesque—
tumble off the edge
of her field of vision.

The strike brings dreams
of leading others
towards the North Star's
light, away from the venom
of slavery.
Harriet leads hundreds of slaves
back and forth

over the demarcation line
to the promised land,
gains a bounty
in addition to the scar
on her head.

✠

IV

An enduring polarization between

good and bad aspects of the world is

built on the foundation of body symbolism ...

Dirt, then, becomes a metaphor which

links the self with the <u>outside</u> of the body—

i.e., the <u>skin</u> and its <u>color</u>.

Joel Kovel in
White Racism

Hair

Since he's been old enough
to see it on tiptoe
in the bathroom mirror
my son attacks his hair
with every weapon barbershop
and drug store can provide.
He slicks his soft black curls
down into a flat mat
glistening like beaver fur.
Then he shaves it
to bristles sharp as pins.
He bleaches it Day-Glo orange.
He carves his head,
sculpting little lightning bolts
over his brows,
the peace sign
into the nape of his neck.
He tries to grow it long,
Jimmy Hendrix wild.
When it won't frizz
into an Afro,
he works his scalp
into a grid,
each tiny plot of hair
twisted and bound
so he can extend them
with long thin braids,
cheap ones
that come in plastic bags.

Exhausted between bouts
to make himself more
white or black—
not the unruliness of in-between—
he covers his hair
with a hat.
Hats!
Oh, my God,
the hundreds of hats!

Beauty Shops
(Chicago)

Hyde Park—home
      of Nobel laureates, U.S. President,
         feral parakeets,
            Nation of Islam.

I search for beauty shops,
      elusive as exotic birds
         in a rainforest.

Arrows on a wall
      point downstairs
         to a receptionist

who shakes her dreads, says,
      we're booked,
         have no openings for weeks.

Hackles raised
      to get my nails filed
         and polished red,

I find a place
      near the train station,

its plaster murals
      of noble '30s laborers
         vanishing under gang graffiti.

I break open the door, silencing
        the row of magpies
                chattering in their chairs.

The owner speedily nudges me
        to a closet in the rear
                where her assistant

puts down her duster
        with its purple-pink plumage and
                boils my feet and calves red—

two slabs of soft fatback—
        in a plastic tub
                of bubbling gray water.

Burned, pumiced
        to bloody shreds of skin,
                I learn my lesson:

white women like me
        are supposed to ride the train
                all the way downtown
                        for our beauty treatments.

Tomb Figure III

Female Shaman
6th Century Japan
Minneapolis Institute of Arts

Tonight I guard the entry
to the museum gallery,
just as I stood sentry
in another kind of memorial
to revered leaders.
Around my neck I wear a talismanic amulet:
a fang, claw, beads of jade.
As my thick body loses
its waist, hips, and his desire,
I turn inward, drawing strength
from Kwannon Bosatsu's store.
In my right hand I offer up
to the goddess muse
a cup of jasmine and thyme
from the bag of curative herbs
wrapped around my wrist.
You have been patient;
you may now drink. Then,
when you look deeply,
my oval eyes and mouth will open
into the black well
of all mystery.

Makeup

Campus casting call:
>> someone to play
>>>> a lineless black servant
>>>>>> in an Off-Off-Broadway play.

The few women of color
>> at this elite women's college
>>>> in the East, admitted for only

a token junior year
>> from historically black colleges
>>>> in the South,

did not dare play the maid.
>> So a white girl gets the part,
>>>> rave reviews for her mute aplomb,

panned for minstrel makeup so dark
>> she blends with the black velvet curtain
>>>> to Jolson ivory eyes and teeth.

The makeup artist,
>> one of the women from the South,
>>>> helps to lighten her up.

Reflected side by side
>> in the mirror edged
>>>> with theatrical bulbs,

they search for humor, irony
      in pots of paints
            the right shade of brown.

The Color of Hospitals

Shortness of breath, pain
    in the chest.
        This time the doctors say

it's bad enough for surgery
    to bypass his heart's worn-out
        parts.

He waffles, sets,
    then postpones
        the procedure several times.

He tells her
    about his mother's death
        at twenty-six—

they whispered it was race murder—
    from a routine appendectomy
        left to fester from infection.

He tells her
    the truths of Tuskegee,
        black men's syphilis untreated

so white doctors could study how
    their penises flagged
        with ulcerous lesions.

He tells her

    about Gram's gallbladder

        growing stones the size of walnuts

from her peevish refusal

    to set foot in

        the white man's hospital.

When he learns

    his surgeon will be a *brother*

        his heart leaps to consent,

happy a black man

    will hold the knife

        when he goes under.

Boxes

The director of admissions calls
from the college back East.
Your son checked
most of the categories
from the list
of racial and ethnic groupings.
Can you provide clarification,
tell me
what he is?

My family came from Germany,
England, Ireland, Scotland.
His father is African American —
African nation and tribe unknown — also
Cherokee, Choctaw, Chickasaw.

I do not tell him
that when my son was little,
ashamed of the brand of slavery,
he identified with me
and his European ancestry,
then at puberty,
anesthetizing the pains of my labor,
became Black and Native American
like his dad.

My cells beam elation.
My son defied
instructions to
check one.
Once again he acknowledges
my genes!

Driving Mom's New Car

The green and gold tassel dangles
from the rear-view mirror
of his mom's new car.
She put it there, remembering
her own high school days
when guys in DAs and white T-shirts,
sleeves rolled up
over boxes of cigarettes,
hung cloth dice and crucifixes,
hoping to get lucky, or saved.
The cop was idling,
waiting for him
to pull from the curb.

Infraction #1:   Tassel obstructing vision
from the rear-view mirror.

Question: Had his mom been stopped
because of the tassel
as she drove
to work, the gym, the mall?

Answer: No.

Infraction #2:   Lights over the rear license plate
not **white** enough.

Question: Is there a design flaw
in the new Tercel?
Should Toyota be contacted
to correct the problem?

Answer: No.

Infraction #3:	Failure to show driver's license stowed under the front seat.
Question:	Hadn't his dad told him stories of being harassed by the police when he ventured out to the suburbs for corporate meetings? The police stopped him, asked, *Sir, where are you going,* *are you lost?* Hadn't his dad warned him to NEVER, EVER reach towards the glove compartment, back seat, floor when stopped?
Answer:	Yes.

Infraction #4:   *Driving While Black.*

Sphinx

Imagine the Sphinx—
      ancient creature
      with body of a lioness
      and human head.

Imagine when laurel crowned the head
      and made the lioness lie prone,
      turning her every move to stone.

Imagine when the lioness, wounded
      by this slight, severed herself
      from the head and was gone.

Imagine when the head, seeing itself
naked now below the neck,
bound up every human cell
      with notions of forever,
      foreignness, and fame.

Imagine glimpsing the lioness
curled inside the belly
in a dream and sensing
      first joy and then
      pending calamity.

Imagine the primal pleasure of reunion,
only to wake and find the lioness,
like so many others,
        has almost disappeared.

Imagine the lioness.
Then try to answer
        Who am I?
without her
        incomplete.

Victoria Falls, Zambia

Just a tourist.
I have not come
like Livingstone
in search of treasures
or lost souls for conversion.
Yet, looking down
from a suspension bridge
into the *smoke that thunders,**
I touch the rim
of a perfect, fully circular rainbow.
                Here,
with a foot on the ring of color,
a marriage of mist and light,
I find both alpha and omega,
the beginning and the ending,
my bounty
at rainbow's end.

Notes

Page 66: The poem "Harriet Tubman" is based on the fifth of the 31-panel **Harriet Tubman** series of narrative paintings by Jacob Lawrence. Lawrence "tells stories" of African American history and social justice. He researched Tubman's life and wrote the captions accompanying the paintings. While my poem is inspired by painting No. 5, 1939-40, it makes reference to other paintings in the series.

Page 86: "Smoke That Thunders" was the African name for the great falls before the English named them "Victoria."

About the Author

Caroline Giles Banks, born in Boston, Massachusetts, was educated at Wellesley College, the University of New Mexico, the University of Minnesota and the University of Chicago. Dr. Banks is a cultural anthropologist by training and profession and was on the faculties of Luther College in Decorah, Iowa, and the University of Wisconsin-River Falls. Her poetry, written in several genres, is often informed by her anthropological training and research. She is the author of *Warm Under the Cat: Haiku and Senryu Poems*, *The Clock Chimes: Haiku and Senryu Poems* and *The Clay Jar: Haiku, Senryu and Haibun Poems*. Her award-winning poems have been published in numerous anthologies, literary magazines and journals. She lives in Minneapolis, Minnesota.

www.ingramcontent.com/pod-product-compliance
Lightning Source LLC
Chambersburg PA
CBHW081515040426
42447CB00013B/3238